JOURNEY

JEWEL MARIE McDONALD

Order this book online at www.trafford.com
or email orders@trafford.com

Most Trafford titles are also available at major online book retailers.

Printed in the United States of America.

ISBN: 978-1-4669-7650-4 (sc)
ISBN: 978-1-4669-7651-1 (hc)
ISBN: 978-1-4669-7652-8 (e)

Library of Congress Control Number: 2013902362

Trafford rev. 09/02/2014

 www.trafford.com

North America & international
toll-free: 1 888 232 4444 (USA & Canada)
fax: 812 355 4082

FOREWORD

September 22, 2012
Columbus, Ohio

From the Pen of Irene Z. Paramore:

I wish to recommend this trilogy written by my sister Jewel McDonald. It's been a long time coming into fruition. One may ask, why *has it been so difficult to write an autobiographical book?* Well, there are a few reasons why this writing has had to be so carefully written down. No longer do we live in the age where grandma's words were golden and no one would dare question them. No longer do we live in the age when families met around the hearth of the kitchen or in the living room. No longer do we even come together at the old kitchen table for meals. No, we as a society have to some extent moved into an individualistic perspective. More and more we hear, *my space, my room, mine, mine, mine; so* when we read a novel or article which suggest that more than (me) is involved, we as the general public shy away from the novel.

The writer of this life story is not only accurate in words, but also in the feelings that she portrays in her story. One can only write this deep if she were a part of this living and growing up in the 40's, 50's, and the becoming an adult in the 60's. Our family, the

Payne family has a unique story and each of the siblings could easily write their story and pulled altogether would make a complete volume of history and of life of our mother's family. The Payne family, our mother was born a Payne, she married a Payne which made her a Payne twice over.

I myself am writing my version of how I saw things played out upon life's stage and hope will bring honor to her writing as well as validate the message in her book. I wish her well in this endeavor and pray that it will be received and accepted in the manner in which it was written. We bring no harm to any family member or remembrance of any departed relatives, but this was how it was when we were growing up in Columbus, Ohio. Jewel's book ventures out more for her being the eldest somehow gives her the title of one who travelled from the family dwellings before the other siblings.

However, see this and know that it is true and well thought out and each word means so very much to her.

To my Sister Jewel: May God continue to bless you and keep writing. There's so much more that needs to come forth so that all the family will know their heritage.

Your fellow writer and Sister,
Irene,
Irene Zenolia Paramore

PROLOGUE

Mother's Day (2012)
Written by Jawharah (which means Jewel
in Arabic) I. Muhammad
Granddaughter

Nana.

I could write for days about the love and bond we share! Just thinking of it puts a smile on my face. And, only the two of us understand it; but that's okay!. I'm so thankful to God for granting me the privilege and great honor for mom and me hold up and I plan on doing just that. I could never repay you for all the comfort, guidance, joy, and love that you've blessed me with. You are and always will be my favorite person in the world. You are my angel. I know this and I love you for it always. Remember, *I love you a bushel and a peck a hug around the neck, a barrel and a heap, and I'm 'talkin' in my sleep, about you!*

Future Teachers of America

Row 1 - Jewel Williams, Beverly Beeton
Carolyn Smith, Joy Edwards, Betty Jo Ruc-
ker, Mary Kostender, Betty Bruce.
Row 2 - Miss Fry, Barbara Chavous,
Shirley Davis, Gloria McDaniels, Barbara
Weaver, Marilyn Morrell, Barbara Duren.
Row 3 - Gloria Hutchinson, Mattie
Summers, Joyce Searles, Dorothy Weakley,
Pat Newlin, Barbara Sanders.

ACKNOWLEDGEMENTS

This work is the product of a lifelong journey. There is no way that I can list all the wonderful people and extraordinary circumstances that have led and accompanied me on this journey. It has taken more than three years to accomplish my goal, however; it has been a joyous and healing task. I would especially like to express my deepest gratitude to Irene Paramore, my sister and fellow writer. Not only for her words of encouragement, but also for sharing her ideas and editing skills.

To my other brothers and sisters Blonzetta Evelyn Delbert and Lamorris without you in my life the quilt that is jewel's journey would have been missing some very important squares.

Special thanks go to my special brother and sister in this faith walk, Doctors Moriba and Barbara Kelsey. Without their valuable insight and knowledge, this project could not have been completed.

On January 4, 2012, Barbara wrote these words:

Dear Jewel,

Our bond of Sisterhood and friendship has developed over more than fifty years. What a blessing: You have always been there for me and I have been there for you! I dedicate this special acrostic poem to you:

Just
Enduring
Willing
Empathetic
Love

Your Soror,
Barbara Kelsey

As I acknowledge those persons who spoke into my life as my work neared completion, I want to extend my deepest appreciation to one of my of closest friends, Patricia Bohannon (AKA PAL).

When Bobby died I don't know what I would have done without my friend PAL. She was by my side constantly, often anticipating what I needed before I did. Even though life now requires that we no longer live around the corner from each other, we are still only a prayer and a "phone" call away. her name is Patricia Bohannon, but everyone calls her PAL. Not only is she my sister-friend, but she will always remain my special PAL.

I would also like to acknowledge my Pastor: Richard E. Spann and my church family: THE MEMBERS OF Kennesaw Avenue Missionary Baptist Church of Marietta, Georgia for their continued encouragement and prayers. Pastor Spann, I will always remember what you told me: that no matter how far away I moved, You will always be my pastor. Thank you and God Bless!

`As I acknowledge those who contributed to the completion of my book, I want to give special thanks to my daughter Caryn Muhammad who has been an outstanding editor. She has also taken on the responsibility of the marketing process. My deepest gratitude also goes to my oldest grandson Rasheed Muhammad who as an eighth grader is already an accomplished artist. I am certain that his design of the front and back cover of the book will be well received.

Finally, I would like to acknowledge my publishers, Trafford Publishing Company. Their willingness to accept my initial effort has been very encouraging.

COBB COUNTY SCHOOL DISTRICT
Human Resources
"Professionals Serving Everyday Heroes"

You Made a Difference!

*The Cobb County Board of Education cordially invites
you and a guest to attend a retirement luncheon in your honor.*

*To recognize and thank you for years of
dedicated, faithful service to the
Cobb County School District,
your presence with a guest is requested on*

Monday, May 2, 2005

DEDICATION

First giving honor to God, who is the head of my life, I dedicate this first telling of my life's journey. For it has only been through His grace and mercy have I come through the many trials and tribulations that I have faced. To my family for their continual love and support, I want them to know that without them this could not have happened.

I would also like to dedicate my first book to Nasir and Malaan Muhammad who are my two younger grandchildren and the lights of my life. They are talented, writers and artists. Am I blessed with a talented family or what?

Little Rock, Arkansas (60 years later)

IN THE BEGINNING
PART THREE

March 8, 2011

INTRODUCTION

Fannie Zenolia, Carrie Ruth, (CAR RU), and Jewel Marie—journeys that are interwoven like a quilt stitched together with gentle hands, square by square—there is soft yarn between each piece holding together the fabric (and stories) of their lives.

"HANDMADE QUILTS"

"Take a look at all the colors of a handmade quilt. Examine the intricate stitches. In some ways, the body of Christ is like a quilt, lovingly stitched by the Lord. May we, like that quilt, be a thing of beauty to a watching world"! (Author Unknown)

"Mom Payne", (Ms. Fannie Z.) born in Baton Rouge, Louisiana, 1897—high cheek bones, amazing eyes that were gentle when she saw me skipping down the street to 173 Talmadge, fiery when she thought that you had done something to one of her children. She was African American and Native American and when she spoke her rich heritage emerged. Her first "Girl Child" was (My mother), Carrie Ruth the Love Child of "Doc" Payne's "Mellow Sax."

"MEMORIES OF "MOM PAYNE"
WRITTEN BY:
JEWEL MCDONALD
MASTER'S PROJECT
WRIGHT STATE UNIVERSITY—1989
-EXCERPT

"The Sunday morning that she died, she was up getting ready to go to Church. (The old Gay Street was now Tabernacle Baptist Church). Mom Payne traveled to such places as Chicago, New Orleans and Los Angeles. (I understand more and more why I can't 'STAY PUT')."

Instead, on this cold February morning, she took her last journey, and as our family writer, Irene wrote in her poem,"

"MRS. FANNIE Z. HAS GONE ON HOME TO BE WITH THE LORD, COULNDN'T WAIT HERE NO LONGER;

"JUST HAD TO CATCH THAT MORNING TRAIN. SHE LOVED TO TRAVEL THAT WAY YOU KNOW,"

WHEN EVER SHE WENT TO AND FRO, AND SO HER LAST TRAIN WAS ABOARD THAT GRAY AND SILVER TRAIN WHICH CARRIED HER STRAIGHT TO THE HEAVENLY GATES."

"Precious Memories, how they linger, how they ever flood my soul." These words are from a hymn learned in my childhood, written by **John Braselton Fillmore Wright** (1920). The memories are of a time in the early 1950's, when a little girl, on a warm summer evening could be seen sitting on the old porch swing with her best friend and confidante. As the movement gently swung them back and forth, her grandmother's smooth, chocolate voice hums, "Work For The Night Is Coming!" This hymn was written by **Anna Louise Walker Coghill**, (1854) The scriptural reference for the song Is John 9:4 (*I must work the works of Him who sent me, while it is day, the night cometh, when no man can work*).

I wondered why she hummed this hymn so often. Was she aware that soon some days would come that seemed so dark that she couldn't work, couldn't sing her song, couldn't even pray.

Even though I know that you shouldn't have favorites, I always knew that I was her favorite grandchild. Perhaps because I was first, and look much like my mother, but more than likely because she knew that I loved spending time with her.

I wondered "is it the fragrance of the lilac bushes outside my window, or is it the memory of Mom Payne that seems to wrap me in its gentle arms".

THE GENEOLOGY

It was the beginning of Spring—March 10th, 1923, when Carrie Ruth was born. Three older brothers rushed home from the cotton fields to rock their new baby sister in her wooden cradle.

She was a sweet child with wise eyes. Did she already know that in a few years she would leave the sweet lullabies behind to sing a new song, a song that was sometimes happy, sometimes sad, but always hers.

Jewel Marie was born on a farm in Marianna, Arkansas—December 31, 1936, maybe in the same room that her thirteen year old mother was born. The cotton fields were bare, the winds were cold and frost was in the air. One journey was ending and a new one was beginning. The old year was leaving and in a few moments everyone around the world would be shouting, "Happy New Year". She was CAR RU'S first girl child. The colors were not yellow and green, (and both girl children cried!)

(Fast Forward):

The year was 1989, Another March, in freezing weather we drove to Marianna, Arkansas to bury Mom's oldest brother, Uncle James, "The Preacher,"

Was Carrie Ruth remembering her life of years ago as we crossed through Memphis, almost to her birthplace. Sometimes I wonder how my life would have been had Daddy Payne not sent for my mom that cold winter of 1941 to come to Columbus, Ohio, the "Promised Land". I met new cousins and realized that I would probably talk, think and live like them. I'm happy that we met, I am so thankful to Daddy Payne for wanting us to live with him.

Jewel Marie
The Stolen Childhood:

How could the girl child tell her mom about what happens when she's not home? Would it stop if she told her or would she get in trouble.

Maybe she knows about those hands that were always touching, but was she afraid of the hands as well. Books became her windows to the world. When she walked to the library alone, it was a time of comfort as the magic in the stories helped her through the times of sadness and pain. Jewel Marie, shielding her younger sisters from the sadness and pain.

Car Ru, a friend, a confidante, a mother, she can't find out what goes on while she is at work.

The oldest, she has to clean and cook dinner before mom gets home from a hard day on her knees cleaning houses in Bexley or Worthington.

The younger ones had chores, but they were sent outside to play where the scary eyes and touching hands can't find them.

Please God, maybe today will be the last day to be afraid to be alone in the house.

(The secret was finally told to someone who promised not to tell," please don't tell", she said, Please don't tell). Car-Ru will be in danger: but when the hands stopped, I knew that "Mom" knew. "Oh God, please protect her from the hands".

Not until years later did we find out that the hands had started touching the younger sisters.

Now as I'm listening to _"Lord I Wonder What Will Tomorrow Bring"_, and _"The Lord Sits High and Looks Low"_ I finally realize why the Holy spirit guided Myrtle to give me those songs to sing. Even as a twenty year old I knew as one of the lines says, _"This is a mean world to try to live in. Can't go no where, got to stay right here until I die."_

Every since that day long ago on Talmadge, when I needed to get the screen door opened and God opened it, I knew that He was my only father. I never knew my biological father, never even knew his name. I had no one to hold and protect me.

I started walking and talking with the Lord when I was six or seven years old and so when I sang these songs, I already knew, _"His helpless children he sees and He cares,"_ _"He knows everything you need"_.

The happiest times for the first girl child were the weekends which included walks to the library and the art museum alone. No eyes watching, no hands touching, no little sisters to take care of, no dinner to cook, _Car Ru was home_. _"Here's a quarter for ice cream or a candy apple. And be careful"_.

She understood that there was a need to just be alone—just the girl child and her thoughts and dreams. Many years later, when secrets were revealed, tears were shed for a childhood that never was.)

Blonzetta Delores

Just a few months younger, but so different. Like her name, Blonzetta Delores, so unique.(My Sister, my friend, my confidante) We have never met anyone else with her name. She has such a sweet, joyous spirit always able to help others smile through their tears. "Praise God" that she came into my life to provide so much joy through the years,

As a teenager, she had her own style and grace. She had the flair of a model and "WOW" can she wear a hat. You can't describe her without mentioning the "Regalettes. These were her friends who had her same free spirit and at East High School, they were recognized for their creativity and ability to stand out in a crowd. They were all "Cute and Popular" so all the other girls wanted to be in there group, but you had to have that special "Something" to belong.

This style and grace are found in her home The colors always spoke of her individuality. When she put them together, you thought of Paris and high fashion. We did convince her to go into her own decorating business, she could do beautiful flower arrangements and she did catering for a few years, but the most special gift that she gave was our first nieces and nephew to spoil and of course we did.

Irene Zenolia

Irene Zenolia, was the youngest of the three girls who sat on cardboard suitcases as they crossed the Mississippi River on their way to the "Promised Land".

A few years ago, what a thrill it was to be in the audience to enjoy her first Original Play, "**The Life of Ms. Ann Spenc**er", as it was sponsored by The Junior Guild of Columbus, Ohio and performed in the perfect setting of a beautiful garden on a warm Sunday afternoon. That was just the beginning.

Today, years later, she has become a Literary Artist, having written several short stories, poems, eulogies and plays. Over her thirty year career, other plays have been performed at churches and her stories are read in many Columbus Public Schools and as far as Cobb County Georgia.

Recently she was nominated for induction into the **Columbus Arts Council!**

We knew when she was a little girl that God had special plans for her. We were not surprised when she told of the call on her life to be a minister of the gospel. Even though she was led to receive degrees from the Trinity Lutheran, and Methodist Theological Seminaries, she has been preaching through the way she lived all of her life.

173 TALMADGE STREET
COLUMBUS, OHIO
1941

Faces are glued to the windows of the train that was taking us miles away from the cotton fields of Arkansas. This became the first of many rides on trains, buses, street cars, and air planes. Daddy Payne was waiting for us at 173 Talmadge Street.

It was our first time having an upstairs and downstairs, but there was no inside bathroom. It was very scary going to the out house at night.

Auntie Alma Grace, (Daddy Payne's sister) lived across the street at 176 Talmadge with Uncle Smiley. I remember that Uncle Smiley was the first person that I had ever seen that didn't have any teeth. I loved going across the street to sit in Auntie's warm kitchen and eat apple and peach cobbler.

Auntie Alma Grace had a great sense of humor: Once when we were in our early twenties and thirties, living on 374 Kendall Place; This was also the time of a rare visit from GREAT-GRANDMOTHER ALABAMA PAYNE: we were doing what we did when the family got together- PLAYING BID WHIST:

This included sisters, brothers, cousins, aunts and uncles. ALL OF A SUDDEN AUNTIE ALMA GRACE WAS AT THE TOP OF THE STAIRS, AND WE HEARD EVERYBODY, IS DOWN HERE! MAMA, COME ON DOWN! CARDs AND DRINKS WENT FLYING EVERYWHERE! UNDER COUCHES, CHAIRS, BEHIND THE WASHING MACHINE AND DRYER! AUNTIE

ALMA GRACE WAS LAUGHING SO HARD SHE WAS IN TEARS, AS WE FIGURED OUT THAT IT WAS ALL A JOKE!

Her granddaughter Melinda and I enjoy remembering those happy times whenever we get together.

One night, something woke me up, and as I looked out the front window, I could see Auntie Alma Grace on the ground in the middle of Talmadge Street, rolling over and over.

As I continued to watch, it became clear that she was fighting someone and it looked like She was winning. Mom made me go back to bed, but the story goes, that a woman had threatened to kill her son Osa Lee, but Auntie jumped in. When I overheard, everybody whispering about it the next morning, it seems that Auntie won the fight and the woman was last seen running down Talmadge Street, with her clothes in her hand.

Auntie Alma Grace was a very spiritual woman and really had a strong alto voice, however, don't mess with her folks. You might find yourself in the middle of Talmadge Street late one Friday night.

Many Saturday mornings you could see four sets of hands of different sizes linked together like soft yarn entwined between squares of a quilt. There was great anticipation as they waited on the corner of Long and Talmadge Streets for the street car. The three girl children and their mother would ride the Street Car from one end to the other(for five cents): During those rides, they would see all the big houses on Long Street and make up stories about what they would do if they lived in them.

(Not knowing that one day they would be the people living in the big houses on other streets, in other cities).

When we visited 173 Talmadge Street recently, a vacant lot was all that remains. Sitting in the car, tears rolled down our cheeks as the memories pierced our souls. However, we could almost hear the familiar voices as they called: Olly, Olly in free new cucumber!

HIGHER LEARNING—A WAY OF LIFE: SEPTEMBER, 1954—

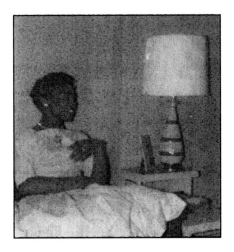

Ohio State University was only the beginning of my love affair with higher learning. It was a roller coaster ride that led to a Bachelors Degree in Education.

Thanks to Mrs. Wilhemenia Kinsey, at East High School, I was awarded a four year scholarship to the Ohio State University, (which was almost unheard of in the 1950's for a little black girl from McCoy Street).

Living at home had its ups and downs dealing with family drama and trying to study was a challenge in itself. Being first in my generation to go to college, (Car Ru) was so proud of her first girl child and was always there to help smooth some of the rough roads. Just like the Talmadge Street experience, The Lord, pushed up the latch on the screen door every time.

After church on Sundays, my other family, placed quarters, dimes and nickels in my hand for bus fare and lunch money.

During my junior year, my best friend (Gwen Lynch) and I pledged Delta Sigma Theta Sorority Inc. After attending rush party after rush party, we began a journey that has lasted for fifty five years. Being a part of this great Sisterhood has created many opportunities, and opened doors all over the world.

Bachelor of Science Degree: Education; Mother,
Brothers, Sisters and other family members

Being a life learner had always been my goal, so that when the opportunity presented itself (1970's) to attend Case Western Reserve University and John Carroll University in Cleveland, Ohio, All I could say was. "Sign Me Up". Then, God placed me in the right place at the right time to receive a Minority Scholarship at Wright State University, Dayton, Ohio, where I received my Masters Degree.

These words that are found in Ecclesiastes, (3:1)

"There is a Time and a Season for All Things"!

Rewind to September, 1958, with my diploma from Ohio State University in hand, I left the tiny Madison Avenue apartment. There was only a short walk through Franklin Park to my first teaching

13

assignment. As they were building the new Maryland Park Elementary School, I would secretly pray that God would allow me to begin my teaching experience in this beautiful place.

Even though I was only teaching one afternoon kindergarten class, my prayers were answered and I was on *cloud nine*. During a recent visit to the old neighborhood, we drove by that corner. There were no voices coming from the playground. Tall grass covered a lonely swing and only the poles were left of the slide where long ago screaming children enjoyed the scary descent then running back to climb up the ladder for another thrill. Looking over at the pool there was no clear blue water glimmering in the sunlight—only faint voices from long ago.

TALMADGE CONTINUED:

"At the other end of Talmadge Street was Mt Vernon Avenue. It was a completely different world From Long Street. On the left hand corner was Garfield Elementary School, the school of our childhood. Now it has become a Museum that houses art and hosts Black History Receptions. Those of us who learned to read there still hear in the distance, Mrs. Mays, my First Grade Teacher, as she tapped on the chalkboard with her pointer, and we "sounded out the words"!

Recently we attended a Kwaanza Celebration there. The large auditorium was brightly decorated in red, black and green. There were no longer any rooms where teachers stood at the doors waiting with great anticipation to impart their 'Gems of Wisdom' to future teachers, doctors and lawyers. As I sang, ***Umoja, Umoja, celebrate Umoja,*** my soul wept for the little girl who didn't have a childhood.

At recess time, the happy voices of singing "Olly, Olly, In Free, New Cucumber" signaled a game of Hide and Seek on the playground and children in red, blue and green coats could be seen piled on top of each other on a winter day singing "Sally on the Saxophone, Keep me warm"!

On the right hand corner of Mt Vernon Avenue, was the drugstore that gave free ice cream cones for good grades. (It was homemade ice cream made from scratch). Auntie Alma Grace had a popcorn stand next to the drugstore. It was a great place for her because she could keep an eye on us in case we got into trouble. Until we were teenagers, we were not permitted to go further than the drugstore without an adult because of—"THE BUCKET OF BLOOD"

As you walked down Mt Vernon Avenue, there was a five and ten cent store where we could spend fifteen cents and have quite a few treats. Then there were the farmer's markets lining one side of Mount Vernon Avenue. I still have the pleasant memories that we spent with our Mom on Saturday mornings as we walked slowly along sampling red grapes and pound cake.Those are memories are of the sights, sounds and smells Of fresh fruits, vegetables and fresh baked cookies and cakes while on right across the street is THE BUCKET OF BLOOD.

It was really a night club that had the reputation, according to Uncle LaFollette and Uncle Melvin of running red with blood on Friday and Saturday Nights. They told stories of all the fights that broke out, shootings and stabbings so that we were afraid to even walk by.

Years later, as adults, my friend Myrtle and I decided that we were brave enough to go in. We were dressed up in our party clothes and as our eyes became accustomed to the dimness of the room, we saw people sitting at tables laughing, drinking, and appearing to be having fun.

We sat nervously at a table by the door so that we could make a quick exit if a fight broke out and blood started flowing from one of the buckets. After about an hour, we left finally realizing that "The Bucket of Blood" was just their reputation not the real thing after all—Not one Bucket.

GAY STREET BAPTIST CHURCH
(THE 1940'S TO THE 1960'S)

Gay Street Baptist Church was located on the corner of Gay Street and Washington Avenue. It was the hallowed grounds of my Baptism and Conversion to Christianity. Gay Street Baptist was a sanctuary where as a young woman I was loved, and nurtured.

The worship services were full of joy as we clapped and sang familiar hymns and gospel songs. Every first Sunday morning we recited the Ist Psalms, which reads in part Blessed is the man that walketh not in the counsel of the ungodly, nor standeth in the way of sinners, nor sitteth in the seat of the scornful". To this day, this remains one of my favorite Psalms.

On the corner of Broad and Washington stands the Columbus Art Museum. It was the place for the young people from church to meet after church, to hold hands and walk around looking at paintings, a safe place where parents did not have to worry about what could happen.

No matter where I've traveled throughout these many years, I have always searched for the museums. So many that I can't remember them all, but some include: "The Science Museum" in Toronto, Canada, "The Smithsonian" In Washington D.C. "Madam C.J. Walker Museum" in Indianapolis, Indiana, and most recently the Apex Museum in Atlanta, Georgia.

It only took about twenty minutes to walk to church from McCoy Street. During winter storms, everyone stayed all day. Each family brought covered dishes which we shared after church. Fried chicken, candied yams, collard greens, cornbread, and cobbler were always on the menu.

I loved the three o'clock afternoon services when guest choirs from other churches were invited to sing an A&B selection. Some choirs came in their fanciest of robes, and others came with white blouses and black skirts. It was not a competition, but each group sounded better and better. On familiar songs, the congregation was on its feet, clapping and singing along.

After the afternoon services we had Baptist Training Union at five o'clock. When we had Evening services, they began at 7:00 P. M. During these special "Programs", we learned to sing <u>"Lift Every Voice and Sing,"</u> <u>(The Negro National Anthem)</u>, which we sang every "Fifth Sunday Night and any special occasion in between. This song was written by <u>James Weldon Johnson</u> and music by his brother, <u>Rosemond Johnson.</u> Through the years, this special song has become a symbol of "Freedom and Pride" for all African Americans.

The Gay Street Baptist Church of the past is no longer there. I was a nineteen year old junior in college, when I had the opportunity to attend my first "NATIONAL BAPTIST CONVENTION".

I had been teaching Sunday school since the age of fifteen and it was quite an honor to be chosen for such a great event in the Baptist Church Life. It was held in Los Angeles, California. This trip became my second train ride—three days and nights-and the loss of my luggage. Fortunately Cleo Wooten and I were the same size so that we shared clothes until my luggage was finally located. Every summer after that, we headed to the "National Baptist Convention. (Cleo is at home with the Lord now), but I still pull out the old "Black and White" photos that hold so many memories).

The convention was held in Buffalo, New York the next summer and we stayed with Aunt Clara and Uncle Bob.

He was a business tycoon and when we walked down the street with his ever present cigar, we felt like celebrities. You heard, "Hey Bob, How's it going?" Everyone knew Uncle Bob.

We discovered that it is really true that opposites attract. Aunt Clara was quiet, not saying too much, with a sweet spirit. She was always cooking and made sure that we had everything we needed to go to church on Sundays.

The most memorable event of this visit was when Irene and I were standing at the bottom of the stairs, getting ready to climb up the steps, and who walked down but "Dr. Martin Luther King Jr. To our surprise we were standing on either side of history as he stood in the middle with his arms around our shoulders. If this had happened in this day and time, I would have been able to record this special event on my camera-phone.

One of the blessings of going to the National Baptist Conventions was the nurturing that you received in the classes composed of people of all ages from all over the United States. Not only did we learn the" THE DYNAMICS OF SUNDAY SCHOOL GROWTH", but we were taught Black History from many who lived it. We didn't even have a camera.

We actually drove all the way to Denver, Colorado the next year. We were excited about such a long ride where we would be stopping at interesting places to eat, visit, and shop. It was amazing that we could stand anywhere in the city and look up at the snow capped mountains. Brother Copeland did all the driving, but his most important job was to stand guard as young men from other cities and other states flirted with the lovely young ladies from Ohio. He's in his eighties now, and every time that I see him I remind him of how well he did his job.

The convention in Memphis, Tennessee was the last one that I attended from the "Old Gay Street". The story about what happened when we stopped at a gas station to use the restroom, changes every time it's told and it also depends who is telling the story. The "Colored Restroom of course, was around behind the gas station, in the dark. As I remember the incident, I was extremely hesitant about going around back because of my experiences with outdoor toilets, and the stories that I had heard about the "KU KLUX KLAN". "I was determined not to use the "Colored Restroom".

Rev. Copeland, having grown up in Georgia, realized the trouble that would be caused had I actually tried to use the "White Only Restroom, Instead, Rev. Copeland took my hand and walked me around back keeping us all safe. I confess that you'll have to talk to him to get his version. It's just a little different from mine.

Just as we had stood in line to shake Dr. King's hand in Buffalo, after hours, there he was standing right in front of us again in Memphis. After he shook my hand, I swore that I would never wash my right hand again. (When I told that story to my Kindergarten and First Grade classes, they would ask, "Have you really not washed that hand again"?, This demonstrates the sincerity and honesty of young children.

"Childhood Memories"

Building snowmen in the winter, having picnics in the park or just sitting quietly reading books, you wondered what made for such a strong bond. Just as the mother lioness watches over her cubs, licking their faces gently, Car Ru ever hugging, or quietly scolding, always loving. It's sad that she couldn't protect us *from the wolf that was at our door.*

These were the three girls who eyes were glued to the windows as they made that long train ride across the <u>Mississippi River</u>. A new life had begun a life that would never be the same. (Only the love of the young mother kept rough waters smooth).

Below is an excerpt from an unfinished story by my sister Irene.

"WILL THE REAL ELIJAH PIERCE PLEASE COME FORWARD"

BY IRENE PARAMORE

PREFACE

"We were privileged to be among the youth growing up in the Gay Street Baptist Church family where the Rev. Pierce was also a member."

"Excitement of Rev. Pierce's picture giving: "I remember Rev. Pierce, a tall, lanky fellow, coming into the door of the church with a picture wrapped in brown paper. He was always trying to surprise someone with an original carving.(This was an idea that took form and shape under the guidance of the Holy Spirit.}

"The whole church would wait in anticipation for Rev. Pierce's turn in the worship service. He would call forth a member of the congregation. What made these gift givings so special was that he had a message for the individual which he said was a message from the Lord".

"I remember when he gave my sister Jewel her carving. We were all surprised as he called her up in his soft voice. (At this time she and I worked in the Primary Sunday School Department and by this time Jewel was teaching in the Columbus City School System).

"Her carving was called *"Suffer The Little Children To Come Unto Me"*, and it depicted Jewel surrounded by children with Christ in the center."

"THIS CARVING IS NOW ON DISPLAY IN THE NEW YORK MUSEUM OF FINE ART TO BE ENJOYED BY THE WORLD")

"The Barber Shop where Rev. Pierce cut hair in the front and carved in the back is no longer standing, but there are still fond memories of sitting on his old stool, drinking COCA COLA that we could get for five cents out of his big red cooler. During a recent visit to the High Museum of Art in downtown Atlanta, I was surprised to see one of his carvings displayed with other "Self-Taught Artist. A statute of Rev. Pierce now stands on the corner of Long Street and Washington Avenue in the exact spot where the barber shop stood. Each time we pass by it reminds us of the quiet preacher whose sermons were within each of his carvings.

MILTON "DOC" PAYNE

Continued:

Daddy Payne waited for me again many years later in a hospital room. Yellow Springs was only an hour from Columbus, but on that day the drive took an eternity. (Somehow I knew that he was getting ready for his final journey)

Yellow Springs, a small village nestled in the Miami Valley, was described as a breath of fresh air. Children played safely outside, doors were left unlocked, no hustle and bustle, so different from our life in the big city of Cleveland. Yellow Springs is the home of Antioch College where Coretta Scott King could be found walking around the campus in 1950's. Yellow Springs was not only a safe haven for Runaway Slaves on the Underground Railroad, it was also a safe haven for runaway souls from big cities all over the country. God allowed this small village to enter our lives for (*such a time as this*).

I taught in Dayton and Springfield, Ohio, but coming home each evening to the small village of Yellow Springs, nurtured my soul

Now I've traded Yellow Springs, Ohio, for Kennesaw, Georgia. There are many similarities, when you visit the small shops downtown, but so different with its history of slavery and the Civil War.

Finally arriving at the hospital, I touched Daddy Payne's sweet face and he opened his eyes for the last time. I felt the loneliness of missing him already, but there was peace knowing where he was going. (For him, there would be no more trips to see the Kansas City Monarchs Play, but his picture is immortalized in a mural on the walls of the Negro Baseball Hall of Fame Museum). Now he is playing his "Mellow Sax" in God's Heavenly Band" *"JUST OVER IN THE GLORY LAND" "THERE WITH THE MIGHTY HOSTS HE STANDS" JUST OVER IN THE GLORY LAND"*

God used the occasion of our first Family Reunion in Kansas City, Kansas to allow us to discover Daddy Payne's picture in a mural displayed on the walls of this famous museum. As members of the family gathered around, the image and basked in the moment, with tears in our eyes, we wondered if Daddy Payne ever knew that he was there among great baseball players.

We concluded that he probably never knew and as a traveling musician, he had been invited to enjoy a Sunday afternoon with friends .Who would know that sixty years later, that his grandchildren and their children would pay homage to him in this Sacred Place. Recently I found a journal entry made during a writing class while working on my Masters Degree at Wright State University.

April 17, 1989:

Today is my grandfather's birthday Last year on April 16, we buried him. If he had lived, he would have been 85 years old. I really miss him. He was a great musician, the first black to attend Juliard. Even though his saxophone and organ no longer give up their sweet melodies, in our hearts the refrains go on and on.

I wonder if he can hear the songfests that we have each time we gather. One brother blows the trumpet, the other on the keyboards, the rest of us blend our voices. I guess we're his legacy, the song he sang to my grandmother in their youth.

GROVE STREET
"UMBRELLAS"
162

199 REASONS TO BE THANKFUL: Compiled by Janice Hanna:
2009 Barbour Publishing Inc.

*This book was given to me by my dear friend—Laverne Suggs-and, I found the greatest definition of an umbrella.

"An umbrella protects you from the elements, keeping your clothes dry and your hairdo intact. In a similar way, God covers us with His love. His blessings, and His provision. He shields us from life's many storms. Scriptural reference:" (Isaiah: 61,10).

On Grove Street, one cool, rainy, Saturday morning, Car Ru needed an umbrella, as she and her oldest girl child walked to the corner store, another journey woven between squares in the quilt. In the store was the lady who lived on the first floor of the house where we lived on the third floor. Unfortunately for her, Car Ru had the umbrella.

All she had to do was apologize for throwing hot water on Irene when she ran through her flowers a few days before. And, she also had the nerve to call her black, nappy headed and said that she had no home training.

The umbrella connected with the lady's head and face in one felt swoop. She jumped up, brushed herself and ran out of the store without a word. Car-Ru was so embarrassed. She kept saying, *I'm so sorry, I broke her glasses, I broke her glasses, I'm so sorry.*

As long as we lived upstairs, we never saw the neighbor from the first floor looking out of her window or standing on her porch again. (Let that be a lesson to you—*Don't call my child names, especially black and nappy headed).*

And as it happened whenever Mom couldn't pick them up, I would get the call,*Can you get your brothers for me?*

Ask my brothers, Morsey and Delbert, about another time that an umbrella played an important role in our lives. I wonder if they remember that rainy day in the 1960's when I picked them up from North Side Day Nursery. I was teaching First Grade at Highland Avenue Elementary School, so often I would get a call from my Mom, "Will you pick up your brothers?"

So, this meant that they would fuss and fight all the way home while I fought the traffic on the freeway.

It takes them to explain how I drove with one hand and without turning around, I could use the umbrella to get in some good licks on their head, shoulders and other body parts.

As an eighteen year old mother of three girls, Carrie Ruth was very protective and very passionate about their well being. Many times you saw them together, shopping or having a picnic.

This was a rare time that Mom Payne came to visit us in East Cleveland, Ohio. After we went shopping at the grocery store, she commented on how I could just write a check for several bags of groceries. I often wondered was she remembering many years ago when it was such a struggle to feed her large family or the years of picking cotton on a farm in Marianna, Arkansas?

"CAR RU"
Daughter, Sister, Mother, Friend

Carrie Ruth Payne, only received an eighth grade public education, but at her death at age seventy one she had a PH.D in life. She chose to begin work at age thirteen cleaning the big houses on the hills to help take care of the family. There were six younger siblings back then on Route Two, Marianna, Arkansas. As the oldest "Girl Child", she chose to place her life on hold. She wasn't aware of the special plan that God had for her life.

She was a born leader, joining Gay Street Baptist Church in 1941 soon after arriving from Arkansas and was there until her Home Going in 1995. She became the first president of the newly organized Young People's Choir, and with her vision a group of young mothers formed the "Ever Ready Club". No one could have known that this would prepare her for a life time in missions.

Her first Missionary Circle was named after a brave woman of the Bible: (The Esther Circle). Just as Esther was chosen for such a time as that and saved her people, the lives of hundreds were saved as "Mom" loved and prayed them through their problems.

One of her favorite sayings was, *There's always enough in the pot for one more!* She never turned anyone away from our door. If you had no place to eat or sleep you were welcomed at our house. Someone once called our house **Payne's Community Center!**

Mom traveled to many missionary conventions over the forty years that she served as Coordinator of Missions and all of her girl children were with her when she was honored with the "Lifetime Achievement Award" from the Eastern Union.

From picking cotton in Arkansas, working on the railroad during the Second World War, in Ohio, to scrubbing floors on her knees, she did whatever it took to take care of her children.

During those years she never gave up on her dream to take the Civil Service Exam. At age fifty she finally had the opportunity and not only did she take the exam, and with an eighth grade education, she had the highest score and was hired immediately by the State of Ohio.

For ten years, mom worked at the Bureau of Workman's Compensation for the state of Ohio, until her retirement. While there, she received many awards and commendations. We were especially thrilled to share in the ceremony when she was honored as the "Employee of the Month".

As stated in the *"Spectrum"*, the monthly publication, *"Carrie is a very dedicated and competent Employee. We call her "MOM". She is always there to encourage us, pick us up when we fall down and give us good advice. Carrie's calming effect is felt in the entire office. More than anything, she keeps people on an even keel."*

When mom was interviewed for the article, she responded

"Callers are often irate at first and must be calmed down. I like talking to people and trying to satisfy them".

Her favorite T-Shirt read, *If I had known that grandchildren would be so much fun, I would have had them first".* Now that I am a grandmother, I know what she meant.

Each one is so different, yet so special. Jawharah is my oldest at age twenty is now a sophomore at Howard University. She's following in her mother's footsteps. Next is Rasheed, who at age thirteen loves being in charge. However; we let him know who are really the bosses in our family. Nasir at age eleven, walks many times in Rasheed shadow but is becoming his own person and Malaan is the five year old princess of the family. Her name means "Beautiful woman in Chinese. And that she is. She has a mind of her own and often shares her opinions about life with anyone who will listen. *I must get one of those T-Shirts!*

CAR RU'S LAST TRAIN RIDE: FEBRUARY 23, 1995

We had been singing hymns around her bedside all day. Her most favorite—"His Eye is On the Sparrow"—as well as "Jesus Told Me That Everything is Gonna Be Alright". We also read her favorite scripture, *I will lift up mine eyes unto the hills, from whence cometh my help, My help cometh from the Lord, which made Heaven and earth: (PS. 121 1-2),* **And then around seven the evening as** *we* **were singing** *"Soon and Very Soon, We're Going to See the King",* **she decided to get on board that train bound for GLORY!**

Through her sobs, I heard my niece Jessica say, *"Get your crown Grandmother".* As I stood on her left side, I saw the last tear slowly coming down her face. I softly wiped it away as I knew that she would soon be waking up in Heaven.

FAMILY ADDITION
1948-1954

ANOTHER PLACE AND TIME"
3119 RINGO STREET

3119 Ringo Street, Little Rock Arkansas, (age fifteen, a young lady), this was the destination of my third train ride. Auntie Alma Grace had chosen me to travel with her to the place of her birth. It was also just a few miles down the dirt road to Marianna, where Car Ru and her Girl Children were born. It took three days and nights—sleeping, waking, looking over the small rail as it wound around and around over the blue waters of the mighty Mississippi River.

As I enjoyed the gentle movement of the train, I had memories of when I was a little girl following closely behind my mother, helping her dig up sweet potatoes and chop cotton. (As a four year old, I enjoyed these chores.) I wasn't aware of what a difficult job this was for a small teenager.

During this visit, I saw Colored and White Restroom signs for the first time. Also, when we took the city bus downtown, we had to pay our fare and then get off the bus and enter again through the back door. Of course, I questioned my grandparents about this strange behavior. What was the purpose of exiting the bus and then getting back on again, why not just walk to the back and sit down. I especially, wanted to see what was different about the two restrooms.

But all that Big Mama Alabama Payne would do was to give me hugs and say, *"That's just the way things are, that's just the way things are".* *But, I kept thinking, "If I ever get a chance, I'm going to sit in the front of the bus and see what happens."* Of course when I grew older, I learned that the only difference between the facilities was in the minds and hearts of the people.

During the 2002 Family Reunion, in our birthplace, we visited 3119 Ringo Street. The house was no longer there, but as we walked around the vacant lot, we could feel the spirits of our ancestors. Since I was the only one of my generation that had visited there years ago, I told the younger ones about hanging clothes on the line in this yard with my great-grandmother ALABAMA PAYNE and sitting on the back porch with great-grandfather SAM PAYNE. Now all that's left is memories.

When we go to the next family reunion, we'll go to Rt. 2, maybe there will still be something there to let me know that this was the place: (Where the colors were not green or yellow, and both girl children cried)

We drove a few blocks and what a wonderful surprise. Cousin Lynette had researched the county records and found the original house build by HARRIET AND ISAIAH PAYNE IN THE 1880'S: We couldn't believe that it was still standing and that people were living in it. They allowed us to walk around in the backyard where we gathered around the old well and sang and prayed

Two hundred descendents led by the eighty year old patriarch Charles Payne, from Kansas City, Kansas, were joyful as they stand once more on this hallowed ground. He listens intently as from his past he hears the voices of the young Milton and Alma Grace, his cousins, as they played on warm summer evenings.

AN INTERLUDE
TENTH AVENUE

This was a small house on a small street that wasn't even paved, but we loved it, after living on the third floor, on Grove Street. Everything was on one floor and one of my favorite photos shows Blonzetta, Irene, and me sitting on the front porch

There was a big backyard with a large pear tree and I always climbed higher than "Sonny", who was six months older than me. It was not far from Ohio State University, which was on 15th Avenue and High Street. An elderly lady named Miss Emma lived with us for a few months. I remember she just showed up one day and then one morning I looked in the room and she was gone. Nobody even mentioned her name. Is this one of those mysteries that adults talked about and often die with the person.

On Saturdays we walked to the Natural History Museum on campus, and then crossed the street to ISALY'S ICE CREAM PARLOR for large cones of all different flavors. During a recent visit, with my friend and Soror Pauline Sheppard, I was pleasantly surprised to see that Isaly's was still there after fifty years.

Since we didn't have a car, we rode the bus everywhere or walked. It seemed like it was a long way to get anywhere, which I didn't mind because I always had a book. The only trip that wasn't fun was (Every Friday) to "DICK'S FISH MARKET". You guessed it._The smell of fish all the way back home, block after block after block.

I usually took this trip by myself, but sometimes Blonzetta went with me. It sounds strange now that an eleven year old could safely ride all the way downtown and back without any problems. Just remember, that was 1947, and I had been helping take care of a family of at least ten people. So I was very willing to get away.

We only lived on Tenth Avenue a short time before Donaldson's Bakery decided to expand and bought our land. This made the way for our next move, which was to McCoy Street, back on the east side.

588/590 MCOY STREET
THE PLACE

The backyard at **590 McCoy Street** became the first of many classrooms. May, 2005, after almost fifty years as an educator, we can hear the sounds of jubilation as hundreds have come to celebrate the end of an era.The Reception Hall at Milford Baptist Church was filled with former students and parents. There were also fellow educators, family and friends from near and far to say *Happy Retirement!* Can you also hear the voices of the more **than four thousand children** who were blessed to be touched by her love?

There was no grass in the backyard of 590 McCoy Street, so the ground became the first chalkboard. It was just before dusk dark on many warm summer evenings with just enough sunlight left to see. A slight breeze was blowing as on all those evenings when three little girls, (Jewel, Blonzetta, and Irene) during a carefree moment used *sticks and stones, not to break bones,* but to embark upon a journey only they shared.

These three little girls who also shared in moments of pain and sadness, can now many years later, over glasses of sweet tea, sometimes smiling, sometimes through tears, remember the backyard of **590 McCoy Street.**

This was such a great journey, from Maryland Park in 1958 to Birney Elementary in 2005.

In the hallowed Reception Hall are former students and parents as well as family, friends, and many, many Fellow Educators. (Most heartwarming of all, were the wonderful students from forty years past, who flew and drove many miles to share this special moment with me).

"Alright students", we hear the voice of their first teacher, the eleven year old girl child, Jewel Marie, in the backyard of 590 McCoy Street. "Let's use the large sticks to draw circles and we'll put small sticks and stones in the middle to make words and numbers."

Then they raced around to the front steps. The two students sat on the bottom step and waited for instructions from their teacher. As each question was answered, they could move up a step and the first one to reach the porch was the winner.

This early beginning was the benchmark of an excellent teacher—these lessons learned long ago on warm summer evenings became the indicators for standards that were integral components for a career that began in the backyard and continued in schools in the North and South.

FAMILY CHANGES
1948-1954

Three girls were soon to become four with the birth of "a beautiful baby sister—Evelyn". She was born during the chill of a November morning. She was so sweet, and easy to spoil. We were older and had after school jobs, so we were forever buying anything that she asked for from clothes to paying for ballet lessons.

At East High School, she followed in her "Big Sister's" footsteps as she played the lead in the musical "Girl Crazy". Of course, I drove all the way from Cleveland to catch the opening show and to surprise her with a dozen roses. We were reminiscing the other day as we shared memories over the phone, about how special she felt to be the only one to receive roses.

Even today when we get together for different family occasions, she still announces that she is the "Baby Sister"!

We spoke recently about the "Mohair Sweater" incident. She had begged all of her older sisters and anyone else that she could corner for a mohair sweater for Christmas. Of course we said it cost too much and she would have to wait until next year.

Of course, the older siblings had planned all along to buy the sweater.

As gifts were being opened, we sneaked hers upstairs and made some excuse to get her upstairs. The next thing we heard was a sixteen year old screaming "Mohair, Mohair", as she is modeling this beautiful pink sweater down the stairs.

Every Christmas someone brings up the "Mohair Sweater" incident.

OH WELL!

We never expected to have brothers, but it finally happened. First Milton Delbert was born and two years later LaMorris.(Morsey) entered our world and nothing was ever the same. The yarn in the quilt was really stretched. There was no longer just sugar and spice and everything nice, but bugs, snails and puppy dog's tails. We were not ready for the daily adventures that were also accompanied by many trips to the emergency room at Children's Hospital to have castes put on broken arms and legs.

THAT'S BOYS FOR YOU

Something else that became apparent as these little brothers developed-their musical ability. They both began playing instruments at an early age. Their careers often took them down different musical paths, sometimes playing together but many times in different parts of the world.

They continue to thrill audiences—with stories from a trumpet, saxophone, or key board that reach back to the legacy of Milton Doc's

Payne's mellow sounds. Mellow sounds that comforted us through times of sickness, sounds that made us smile when we were sad.

I like to remind them from time to time that if it had not been for the part time jobs of their older sisters who paid for music lessons they would not have enjoyed successful careers.

LaMorris traveled for many years as far as Japan and Germany with *Rick James and the "Stone City Band.* He now has his own *production* company and is sharing his knowledge with young people in Columbus, Ohio and surrounding areas Although He has lost most of his eyesight and needs a driver, he still continues to impart sounds from his soul.

He has passed this legacy on to his son Desmond. I understand from the family grapevine that he has already made a Demo C.D. and that he sounds like Frank Sinatra.

Just as our generation sang around the old piano in the living room, our children and grandchildren are carrying on Milton *Doc's* legacy.

"Milton" (Delbert) who was named after "Daddy Payne, is now spreading the joy of music throughout the city of Tampa, Florida. His journey includes becoming the minister of music at several churches in that area. He has formed a small jazz quintet to introduce another part of the world to his sound that began many years ago, in the living room, in the basement or sometimes on the front porch at 374 Kendall Place.

INTERLUDE
Under The Street Light
590 McCoy Street

Our house was the meeting place and our corner was special because it was where the street light was located.

We all started gathering under the street light at dusk dark, teasing, racing around enjoying the last few minutes of "Olly, Olley in free new cucumber".

As the street light slowly evolved like a butterfly from a cocoon—children of all shapes, sizes and colors began to scatter hastily to front steps and porches-up and down streets and around corners. Parents began emerging from screen doors and looking out windows. You were in BIG trouble if your name was called and you were still under the street light.

All families have stories that they tell when they get together for Family Reunions and Holidays: This incident happened when Delbert was four or five years old. We started getting worried about him after he had not come home from across the street at his friend Buster's house for almost an hour. Just as everyone started spreading out around the neighborhood, looking for him, we saw him sitting happily in the red wagon being pulled by our cousin Kenny. Mom was so happy to see him safe that she forgot to punish him for leaving the backyard without permission.

Years later (1954-1958), leaving McCoy Street each day to attend The Ohio State University, I had to take two buses. Depending where my first class was, I would get off the bus at 15th and High Streets and cross the Oval or get off on Neil Avenue and walk around Mirror Lake. On spring mornings, I loved walking around the lake, listening to the Cardinals and watching young lovers studying on the grass. In the winter the lake was frozen and many brave students walked across, however; I never got up the nerve. I kept seeing myself going under the ice and drowning.

During the *Fifties,* there were not many other students on campus who looked like me. Now, I even know a professor personally who taught there. (Richard Moriba Kelsey Ph.D). His lovely wife Barbara and my sister Irene are the same age. Even though she's younger than me, we have become very close especially since she relocated to Georgia. Not only is she my sister in Delta Sigma Theta, she is my sister in Christ.

When Bobby died (9-3-10), Barbara and Moriba were there to offer comfort during my hours of bereavement. It makes the lonely times easier just to know that they are near and I can always call on them. It's strange how history repeats itself. While growing up in Columbus, we lived only a few blocks from each other. Now fifty year later, we again live just a few blocks away.

Now, I watch the Buckeyes play every opportunity that I have. I wanted to go to the games, but they played on Saturday afternoons. I could only listen to the cheers that came from the stadium as I cleaned bathrooms and scrubbed the kitchen floors of the white Fraternity and Sorority houses.

When the crowds spilled onto 15th Avenue, I would join in shouting *Go Buckeyes,* to give the impression that I was coming from the game. I was really going to catch the bus back to 590 McCoy Street or downtown to F. & R. Lazurus Department Store where I washed dishes in the Employees Cafeteria. Even being awarded a *four year scholarship,* in order to purchase books, eat lunch, and pay bus fare, I had to work.

Many times on Sundays, as I was leaving church, quarters, dimes, or nickels were placed in my hands,

Along with encouraging words. Once, a sweet lady, named Lou Carrie Gray, who made the best homemade ice cream in the church, gave me all the proceeds from her weekend sales.

As I look at one of the first black and white Polaroid photos taken way back then, even with frayed edges, I can still see the joy in my mother's eyes as her first girl-child became the first in our family, the first one in our church, and the first one in our neighborhood to graduate from the **Ohio State University.** Fifty years later, many family members have graduated from other colleges, I still remain the first and only one. Also, my commencement was the first to be held at the **new St. John's Arena,** on **Friday, August 29, 1958 at 9"00 A.M.** I recently saw a news bulletin that featured the newly built arena. I wonder how many who look like me have had their commencement ceremonies in the **St John's Arena.** in the past fifty five years.

Now watching the games being played, I notice that most of the players are African American. Fans of all colors and cultures are in the stands. What a difference five decades make.

October, 1957, a special event took place. Twelve young members of the Pyramid Class of Delta Sigma Theta Inc, proudly marched across the **Oval.** They were wearing white dresses and red gloves. Big sisters walked on each side happily displaying the aspiring members of our great sisterhood. Now years later, not only am I actively participating, but so is my daughter who was initiated on Howards's Campus twenty five years ago.

As I have traveled all over the United States, I also had the opportunity to travel to Europe, to Canada, and to the Bahamas I have been blessed to meet members of my beloved sorority in each of these countries. One of my greatest experiences was spending time with the late Dr. Dorothy I Height, who recently took her last journey. She traveled aboard that great train that took her to **Omega, Omega.** Not only was she a great inspiration as my Soror, but also as Founder of the **National Council of Negro Women.**

These were also the years of the **Civil Rights Movement.** Hearing of the **Sit-ins** at the lunch counters, we wanted to travel down south to join the **Freedom Riders,** but our parents would not hear of it.

Instead, we decided to stage a **Sit In on the front lawn of the President's House.** Ours was a peaceful demonstration, not at all like some that you see today. Our demands were for better food in the cafeteria (Instead of the Mystery Meat). The President's wife actually brought us out a freshly baked pie as a peace offering.

A recent visit to a local high school amazed me. As I sat in their cafeteria, I observed all the food choices, ranging from a salad bar to a buffet with many kinds of pizza, entrees, and desserts. Do you think our *Sit In* made a difference.

Throughout the last few years, I have had several opportunities to protest against injustice when and wherever I have experienced it. It appears that I have passed this attribute on to my daughter, who organized the black students in her predominantly white, private school, to fight peaceably against school policies that were unjust.

During her five years at Hathaway Brown School for Girls (H.B.S.) it was exciting to attend her many plays and concerts and support her as she tried to solve the all the world's social and political problems.

Her graduation day dawned warm and sunny, but my emotions were mixed. Was I ready for my sixties love child to go off to her new life at *Howard University.* I cried all the way back to Ohio and for the next two weeks every time I went into her room.

History has a way of repeating itself as Caryn's first girl child, Jawharah, followed in her mom's footsteps. At the age of ten, Caryn traveled to France as a part of one of the first *Study Abroad Programs:* As a student at *The Carver School of Early College,* Jawharah spent several weeks in South Africa, Spain and France. (*But Just Maybe),* her love of travel began with grandmother, her namesake, who's very first airplane flight was from New York to London and then on to Germany. As they say, *The apple doesn't fall far from the tree.*

588/590 MCCOY STREET
THE PEOPLE

588 and 590 McCoy Street was a double which meant two houses attached together. Poppa cut a hole through the wall so that we could go back and forth. It was as though we had one big house. Irene and I

recently counted everyone beginning with "Mom Payne", all the uncles and aunts and cousins and decided that there were twenty seven of us living there at one time.

McCoy Street is now an exit ramp off interstate 71. When Urban Renewal came to town in the 1950's/1960's, it took away our childhood streets, but it paved the way for the move to the beautiful house at 374 Kendall Place.

We had four aunts named Mary, so we attached our uncles names to theirs to make a distinction between them especially at family gatherings: such as: Aunt Mary Oscar, Aunt Mary Ivory, Aunt Mary Johnny and so on.

During my ninth summer, Aunt Mary Oscar had to go to Buffalo, New York, and decided to take me along. The second train ride was different from four years earlier. She bought me my own leather suitcase and new outfits and one that I especially remember is the sailor suit with a coat and hat. I wore it when we went to <u>Niagra Falls.</u>

As children we thought Uncle Oscar and Aunt Mary were rich. When we visited their house, it seemed that we rode a long way, but when we were older we realized it was only about twenty minutes away. Their furniture had plastic covers that stuck to you when it was warm and made cracking noises when you stood up. There were beautiful flowers growing in their front and backyards. When we ate dinner we ate in the dining room with dishes that matched and a table cloth on the table.

Mother's youngest sister was "Aunt LaVera". We thought of her more as a sister than an aunt because she was our same age. After her death, our cousin Dawn Alisa wrote a memorial letter that was simply intitled: <u>"Aunt Vere"</u>

Aunt Mary (Sonny) also known as Aunt Mary Elizabeth was my age and lived across the street from us. She is more like a sister than an aunt. She and Uncle Sonny dated all through high school and married right after graduation. He joined the marines and was so handsome in his uniform. He was six feet tall and she was five feet, so we called them MUTT AND JEFF: God brought him safely back from Viet Nam, and they celebrated almost fifty years of marriage before he passed. *I REALLY LOVED TO HEAR HIM LAUGH!*

Excerpts are:

"Aunt Vere was by far one of the coolest aunts I knew. Her home, on any given weekend was filled with great—nephews and great-nieces, because we were the same ages as her own children. I remember staying weeks at a time during summers in my youth. Even while in the Air Force, home on leave, I would head straight to her house. She was someone you could always call on for help."

"Aunt Vere had a beautiful voice. When I was young, I wanted to sing like her. I loved to hear her sing, "Lift Him Up", It didn't matter what state of mind you might have been in, When she began to sing, "I need somebody to: lift Him. Whatever your problem, you at least didn't think about it during the song.

Because we are a singing family, her voice will truly be missed. As we press toward the mark, to fight the good fight, to finish our race, I know my Aunt Vere is resting in His arms right now, having been lifted to heaven to be with her Lord."

I love you and miss you,
Dawn Alisa (Cochran) Dunn

In the tradition of African American families, whenever anyone came from the south, they lived with the family that had the biggest house until they could afford to move into their own place. Since we had the biggest house, we had relatives moving in and out all the time. All my uncles and aunts had beautiful voices and are now singing in the heavenly choir. The only one remaining is Aunt Mary (Ivory). She must be at least ninety years old.

Auntie Jack was my favorite Aunt. Two years younger than mom, she was witty and so strong. When I would go to her for advice, she would always have a smile and her favorite saying was, *"Everything is going to be alright"*. My sister Blonzetta reminds me so much of her.

Even during the time when her husband Uncle K.T. died from tuberculosis, she was the one who comforted us. It was the first time that I had seen anyone die. He just seemed to fall asleep on the couch. (I kept expecting him to wake up and tell one of his jokes that we never understood and he always laughed harder than anyone else.)

Sheila O'Kelly, Auntie Jack's granddaughter, has her sweet spirit. Sheila was born with a hearing and visual impairment which she has incorporated into a bestselling novel, **"SOMETIMES I JUST FEEL LIKE WRITING"**. She has captured the world of the traditional black church with her collection of poems and short stories taking the pain and struggles of being different to ease the sadness of others.

The chapter, **"WISH I WAS A FLY ON THE WALL,"** was especially amusing. I know that we have all had a time when we wish we had been a fly on the wall, but instead, I would like to include a short excerpt from the chapter: **"GRANDMA DIED TODAY"**.

"The phone rang while I was asleep, I opened my eyes to see the clock. 5:00 A M.

"Hello", I whispered.

"Sheila, this is Mom. I called to tell you that your grandma died today"

"No", I cried out. Not my grandma! Every ounce of grief and pain that was within me came out in long sobs of sorrow. I lay back in the bed. I heard my husband talking to my mother, trying to console her for losing her mother. All I knew was that my grandma had died that day. I cried, moaned, and sobbed.

After my husband hung up, he gathered me in his arms. "Shhh, it's okay." He softly stroked my hair. When I finally stopped crying, I thought, Dear God, what are we gonna do without my gremmie around? Jason came upstairs to our room with tears in his long eye lashes. He uttered not a word.

You must rush out to "Barnes and Nobles" and pick up a copy. I picked up several copies to give to friends. Am I proud or what?

374 KENDALL PLACE
A YARD WITH GRASS AND FLOWERS

The move from McCoy Street to Kendall Place was on the other side of town but seemed like a different world. It was just one big house with bedrooms for everyone. There was even a finished third floor with a bathroom which Irene and I turned into our very own apartment. There was a front and backyard with beautiful grass and flowers in the yard.

I'm looking at the picture with Mom (standing in the backyard) taken on a Sunday after church still wearing her hat and high heel shoes. I t seems that she was just saying, Lord thank you for answering my prayers.

(There is side bar about that picture that still remains a mystery.)

Wydell Gaines who was an amateur photographer at our church took the picture. What we still don't understand is how he was able to switch "Mom" from one side of the yard to the other. We still chuckle about it.

"MY GERMANY EXPERIENCE"

While living on Kendall, I had the opportunity to travel to Germany. With my wandering spirit, this came at a great time. This was the beginning of the "Fly Now, Pay Later Era". I took a six weeks course in conversational Germany and off I was to Germany.

Also, I was trying to find myself after recuperating from my first major surgery which was to determine if I would ever become a mother. I believed that in God's own time, it would happen.

"Will the six weeks of conversational German be enough to get me through all of the adventures that I was planning? My journey included exploring quaint shops downtown Heilbron and ordering Weinistiezel in a local restaurant in Stuggart. (Unfortunately, I can't find any of the pictures)

The memories are all in my heart.

I didn't realize what a celebrity I would be when some friends took me to a local dance in Stuggart. Later I learned that a beautiful African American young lady was a novelty. I enjoyed all the attention from the local gentlemen. With the world as it is now, would I have been found walking around downtown in quaint German villages?

As an educator visiting the local elementary schools was a part of my experience. I learned that schools are called *"Gymnasiums"* and students went to school all year. This was considered innovative in 1961, but 2011 brings the world of *"Charter and Magnet Schools"* and many varieties of alternative education plans so that students may have successful experiences. My own grandchildren have been recipients of excellent educational experiences which have included "Study Abroad" and attending a single gender academy.

(From Maryland Park to Birney Continued)

At this time, I was only teaching an afternoon kindergarten class. In the 1990's, the public school's instituted all day kindergarten classes, no longer were there A.M. and P.M. classes. I had traveled a long road from my *Backyard class of 590 McCoy Street.* I was living in a tiny apartment on Madison Avenue and since I didn't have a car, I took a shortcut across Franklin Park each day. While walking across Franklin Park each day, I often thought about the happy times that we had in the park over the years.

There were the many 4th of July cook outs. Everyone came early to spread their blankets out to save the best spots. We always stayed until dark to watch the fireworks. There was no fear when after the last bright light faded in the sky, hundreds of us walked to our various neighborhoods near and far. Holding hands, voices could be heard singing, little children could be seen as they darted in between families trying to catch lightening bugs. Recently, I asked my younger brother, *Morsey*, if he remembered stepping over into the lake during one of our outings. He was only age three or four, and all of sudden he decided to step over into the lake. We all got soaking wet trying to save him from drowning. His answer was, *It just felt like a fun thing to do.* Through the years, I have learned that the quote, *Walking to the beat of a different drummer,* definitely describes my youngest brother. Later as I talk about his life and his contribution to the world of music, you will understand **why he had to step over in the lake.**

(Meanwhile Back at Maryland Park Elementary School)

I always arrived to work two hours early every day. Even though I only taught in the afternoon, I created beautiful bulletin boards and decorated my room as though the children were there all day. I must have impressed someone, because one day an important person came from downtown at the Board of Education. An afternoon kindergarten class at Highland Avenue School located on the Hill Top needed a teacher. Aunt Thelma who worked at the Bd. of Ed. mentioned my name to the right person. No one who looked like me had ever taught on the Hill Top, however the Supervisor explained *excitedly that integration was coming, we need you to go.* **There will be children of different races learning together for the first time. This would mean teaching at two schools, but we believe that you can do it. As I watched the expression on his** face, I wondered, *what was he really asking?* Just as I was to be the first African American teacher on the Hill Top, years later I would be the first to integrate school staffs in Georgia as well.

The journey at Highland lasted six years with children of different races learning together for the first time. Stitch by stitch, the girl child's patience and love pulls together parents and teachers; many who in the beginning had said that a black teacher could not teach white children. Then it was time for the next journey. *Don't go*, said the parents, on the Hill Top. *Don't go* cried the children on the Hill Top. *Who will produce our school productions,* exclaimed the teachers on the Hill Top, but like Abraham, it was time to go. *By faith he sojourned in the land of promise, as in a strange country, dwelling in tabernacles with Isaac and Jacob, the heirs with him in the promise:* Hebrews 11:8-9. Fast forward to October, 1997, Cobb County Georgia, another time and another place, but someone from the Board of Education came to see me. I was teaching at Big Shanty Elementary school, which was the former site of a famous Civil War Battle. *You have been awarded an AT&T mini-grant for your innovative idea paring high school seniors with your five year olds. What a great idea: Key pals instead of Pen Pals. Project amount was $1,000.00 integrating internet technology into collaborative storytelling.* We were nominated for the Technology &Learning 1998 Teacher of the Year. Can you believe it? On this very spot hundreds of years earlier, slaves were picking cotton.

(Thanks to the principal Carolyn Hall, who believed in me, I became the first African American teacher in Cobb County to deliver Gifted Collaboration to hundreds of children).

Again, God said: *for such a time as this you must go and teach the children! No one looks like you, but I will prepare the heart of the king:* Esther 4:14.

From 374 Kendall Place to 694 120th Street Cleveland, Ohio—The 1960's: (CJG) Caryn Janine Gay

Aunt Thelma was waving from the porch at 694 East 120th Street. *You made it. How was the trip? Call your mother!* Carrie and Thelma were best friends since their young days at Gay Street Baptist Church.

They are together again, singing in the **Heavenly Choir** around God's throne.

Highland Avenue was my last school in Columbus, Ohio and Miles Standish became my first school in Cleveland, Ohio. The two schools were as different as day and night. Miles Standish was located in a unique location. We were able to take neighborhood walks across East Blvd to the beautiful parks where statutes of the founding fathers were located. Just visiting those parks was a history lesson for teacher and students as well. We also watched Lake Erie change from beautiful and serene in the spring and see the frightening waves when winter winds blew.

My Love Child

Caryn Janine Gay, was my sixties love child. She began her journey while I was teaching at Miles Standish. Her season began in the fall when the leaves of yellow, brown and orange were falling from the trees. Autumn has always been my favorite time of the year. It's not like spring when everything is green and beginning to grow. It's not extremely cold like winter when it snows and you stick your tongue out to taste the snowflakes, or like summer's hot sunrays when they send you clamoring for cool dips in the pool.

It was meant to be that our journey together was to begin during my happiest season.

The first of her many learning experiences began at The East Cleveland Montessori Pre-School where she learned to discover and explore.

At age three, how were we to know that seven years later we would find ourselves hugging and saying *Bon Voyage* as she boarded the airplane for Paris France. We were excited yet nervous about her going so far away for twenty days, but proud that she had been chosen along with other Major-Work Enrichment students.

Her horizons were broadened as she lived with a French family, learned to ski and gained an appreciation for another culture. *The Study Abroad Program,* has now spread all over the country, but in the 1960's and early 1970's was a vision of Dr. Charles Jordan who was one of the first African American Supervisors of Education in the Cleveland City Schools.

History has a way of repeating itself as Caryn's first girl child, Jawharah, followed in her mom's footsteps. As a student at The Carver School of Early College-Atlanta, Georgia; she traveled to South Africa, Spain and France. **(But just maybe),** her love of travel began with her grandmother, Jewel, who traveled all over the United States and who's first airplane flight was from New York to London, England, then on to Germany. As they say, *The apple doesn't fall far from the tree.*

Encouraged by my fellow educator, Elizabeth Clark, who is now teaching in a heavenly classroom, Caryn was able to take advantage of the excellent educational experiences offered at Hathaway Brown School for Girls. There were approximately 50 African American students out of the 300 students, however during her five years of attendance, her presence was definitely felt. She helped organize the first *Black Studies Awareness Organization*. It was exciting to attend her many plays and concerts, as we also supported her efforts as she tried to solve all the world's social and political problems. (This reminded me of my Ohio State University marches and sit-ins.

Graduation morning was warm with a slight breeze blowing. (May, 1985). Grandmother Carrie along with many aunts, uncles and friends, proudly watched as forty lovely ladies dressed in beautiful white dresses received diplomas and said *Hello world, here we come.* My emotions were mixed as an old life was ending and a new life at Howard University was about to begin. Excitement for my *Sixties Love Child*, was mixed with not being ready to let her go

Know from whence you came, If you know whence you come, there is no limit to where you can go: This quote from James Baldwin appears in the souvenir calendar From Whence We Come, published at Howard University (Academic year 1988/1989). This was the year that Caryn was Public Relations Director of the Undergraduate Student Assembly. As she prepared to leave Howard and embark upon life's stage, she left these words: For we are so preoccupied with the fulfilling of our materialistic dreams, we have lost sight of our parents and grandparents dreams. All I am asking you to do is pledge yourself to our people and our cause and the rest will fall into place.

Along with the photograph of her in her cap and gown, I also cherish the picture of me standing next the comedian Dick Gregory. From what I understand, he was visiting Howard's Campus for the Homecoming Activities, and of course I couldn't miss this great photo-op as they say.

New York, New Jersey, North Carolina, Georgia, each state was a blank page to write history and bring to life the next generation. While visiting her in New York, she took me to see my first Broadway Play: *Five Guys Named Moe, which I will never forget.* I applauded her as she won awards at the radio station in Wilmington, North Carolina. Now the soft strings of yarn weaving through another quilt, made her life's dreams come true.

From the Backyard of 590 Mccoy
To Classrooms Near and Far:

Captain Arthur Roth Elementary School was named for the policeman who began the Safety Patrol Program for the Cleveland, Ohio city schools. This school was known for its innovative teaching styles and interaction with parents and the community. It was an honor and a privilege to be asked to teach there. It was during the era of *Say it Loud, I'm black and I'm proud! (*James Brown). Wearing a very large afro and dashikis we taught our children about their Black History. Carl Stokes, the first mayor of a major United States city came to visit and shook everyone's hand.

Fifty years later, the building is still standing and is now a Science Academy (one of the first charter schools in Cleveland.) If walls could speak, you would hear the voices of Michael, Harland, Tonya, Dawn, Demetris and little Billy Davis. (Billy could steal your heart with his winning smile—I know that he is smiling down from heaven,(He left us to soon.)

Since that time, I have taught hundreds of students from Capt. Roth to Birney the little known facts about black inventors such as: Alexander Miles who invented the elevator, Sarah Boone, who invented the ironing board, Thomas Stewart who invented the mop, and George Sampson who invented the clothes dryer. I've also had the opportunity to take many young people to museums such as the Harriet Tubman Museum in Macon Georgia and the Apex Museum in Atlanta, Georgia. These museums and several others exhibit the many accomplishments of African Americans throughout the United States that are not well known.

I now look at the pictures of former students taught there who now have families of their own. Several of them flew and drove in from as far away as Maryland and Virginia to attend my retirement reception. They are former five year olds who now live far away from room 105 at the end of the hall. Now I receive Christmas cards, which when I open them I see their children who have five year old faces.

I encouraged my many students to be life-long learners. I have endeavored to be one as well. I had the opportunity to become an entrepreneur and open my own Language Arts Center in the fall of 2006. I attended Kennesaw State University for twelve weeks and upon graduation, I became the founder and owner of **The Carrie R. Payne Center for Language Arts. (LLC).**

Upon completion of my Doctoral Degree in Pastoral Community Counseling, at **Argosy University,** an additional component will be added to the language arts center. My plans are to make pastoral counseling an integral part of the center. Perhaps because I have healed from my **Stolen Childhood,** I will be able to guide others through their **Quest for Peace and Meaning.**

The following is an excerpt from the card given to me by Michael Meadows on the occasion of my retirement reception. Michael, Harland, Tonya, and Dawn who were former kindergarten students really filled my heart with joy when they walked into the banquet hall. The excerpt reads: *It was so great seeing you at your retirement celebration. I felt truly honored to share my feelings about you and what you have meant to so many children over the years. I truly believe that the first years of school set the tone for how a child views education and you gave us all a true love of education and love of ourselves. Thank you for being so special and for treating me the same.*

Singing in the Evangelistic Choir while attending Abyssinia, I met two special women who have remained friends for these past fifty years. They were able to come one from Ohio and the other from Florida to join the celebration of forty seven years of teaching. I'm looking at the picture of us sitting at my kitchen table relaxing after dinner. This poem describes us perfectly. *Friendship is a tapestry woven through the years-with threads of joy laughter, happiness and tears. It's a work of art so priceless, it's shared by precious few, get easily created by a loving friend like you!*

NOW

Come now into this marriage with grace,
For I am standing by your side
I have watched you as you have run your race
In my love you do abide:
I bring you two together now for my glory will

You be as one: an example of my love
And what a marriage should be.
Keep your eyes on me dear ones, and your problems
Few will be . . . If Satan shall tempt,
Peace be assured, in me you'll have victory.
Walking in my Grace, love will abound,
Walk hand in hand with me:
Listen to my voice, in all things, and perfect your
Love will be:

Written 5/20/81 by Tonya McDonald   As inspired by Our Lord God

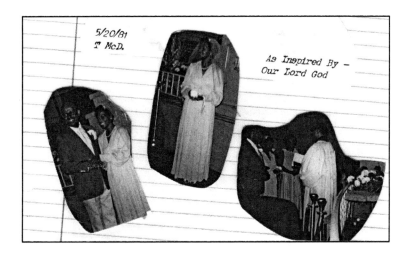

Bobby and I started dating formally after a joint choir rehearsal one Tuesday night at Greater Abyssinia Baptist Church. We knew each other from seeing each other at church and he had been trying to take me to dinner for eight years. When I saw him that night, something in his eyes was different and I accepted his invitation and the rest as they say was history. Our first few dates were always a threesome. We always took Caryn along on our dates. For so long it had just been the two of us and I wanted her to become comfortable with him. We were married almost thirty years before the Lord came for him Thursday morning (9-3-10) at 7:00 A.M. As a driver for twenty five years, for the

Regional Transit System, I was not surprised that his last journey was early in the morning.

In March, 1983, nineteen month old Bobby Junior entered our lives. I wrote a profile of him when he was twelve years old. I started with an acrostic poem about him using the letters in his first name:

Brave
One in a million
Best of all
Believer in Christ
Yearning to learn about Jesus

A partial excerpt of this profile reads: *In the words of Norman Wright the children's author,* every *child is a priceless original.*

I'm just sharing one paragraph from this profile. *Constant movement is also uniquely Bobby especially his feet. He is poetry in motion as he dribbles the soccer ball down the field. Walking down the sidewalk, he dribbles tin cans, rocks or paper cups. Running with the high school track coach, he keeps up with him stride for stride. Bobby's comment to him was, It's not how big you are, it's how fast your feet can go.*

Snow Hill Elementary School is nestled in bosom of Wittenburg University, Springfield, Ohio. This beautiful setting was my educational home for nine years. For most of that time, I was the only African American classroom teacher, however; the principal and Physical Education teacher looked like me. We formed a strong bond that continues even today.

I taught first, second and third grades during my journey there. I was also blessed to form a strong bond with several parents and students who e-mail regularly. On October 12, 1992, one of my many parents wrote a letter that I still cherish. I was being chosen for Teacher of the Year: The letter Reads in part: *To whom it may concern:* **A gentle, melodic voice filled the colorful, the eye catching room. Now class, she said in a soothing manner. We have a special guest with us today. Who was the visitor? She had invited so many to this haven of learning. Likewise, Jewel McDonald exhausted every resource to enhance her whole Language classroom. My son Ben, eagerly pulled on his backpack to travel to Mrs. McDonald's special classroom crowded with curiosity and caring.**

Many parents and friends of classmates shared information on such subjects as: Chinese, French, French cooking, signing and Claude Monet. Let us make it official. Jewel McDonald is an outstanding teacher and should have this title of Teacher of the Year bestowed on her from now until the end of time.

Thank you for your time and consideration: Sincerely, Denise Roberts. Denise Roberts.

October 12, 1992

To Whom It May Concern:

A gentle, melodic voice filled the colorful, eye-catching room. "Now class," she said in a soothing manner, "we have a special guest with us today."

Who was the visitor? She had invited so many to this haven of learning. Likewise, Jewell McDonald exhausted every resource to enhance her whole language style of teaching.

Many parents and friends of classmates shared information on such subjects as Chinese, French, French cooking, Signing and Claude Monet.

My son, Ben, eagerly pulled on his backpack to travel to Mrs. McDonald's special classroom crowded with curiosity and caring.

And so I ask that this soft-spoken, beautiful woman be honored with more than a pat-on-the-back and handshake.

Let us make it official. Jewell McDonald is an outstanding teacher and should have this title bestowed on her from now until the end of time.

Thank you for your time and consideration.

Sincerely,

denise

Denise Roberts

Memories of Mom Payne
Written Assignment/Master's Thesis:
May 13, 1989
Excerpt:

It was always a happy time when I walked to my grandmother's house. Warm sunlight could be seen coming through her kitchen window even on cold winter days. When she saw me approaching, as she always did, I could see the twinkle in her eye and the kind, gentle smile that warmed my heart.

I loved to hug her round, soft body. Her skin was so smooth, with the faint scent of her special lilac cologne. As I savor the fragrance of the lilac bush just beginning to burst into bloom, I am reminded of her love and gentleness. It's amazing the flood of memories that return because of a sound, a touch, or smell.

During this time, another first happened in my career as an educator. It was quite an honor to become a part of the first **Teacher Leader Network in the Miami Valley.** As it turned out, I was the only one chosen from my school district that year. As I reflect upon the qualities that were needed, I still feel proud of what was stated in the category: *Effective and Creative. These teachers create classrooms where students learn and learn to take responsibility for their own learning. Their classrooms are exciting, interesting places where students are involved with subject matter and people. These teachers model learning processes; they model excellence.*

I also had the opportunity to introduce *Whole Language* as a natural way of learning to teachers in my school and throughout the school district. It became a way of life in my classroom and of course, it met with resistance from other teachers and some parents. My principal was very supportive and encouraged me to present workshops to other educators in our school and in the district. In the final analysis, when I left after nine years, there were hundreds of students who were emerged in language through reading, writing, being read to, observing and listening. There were also hundreds of educators who now understood that whole language is a belief system that supported students to have a lifetime of productive and joyful learning. Now whole language is old school, but during the 1990's it was considerer on the cutting edge of educational strategies.

I'm looking at the sweet, beautiful smile on the face of Kate Nelson, who was in my third grade class during this era. The photograph depicts my twenty five students in front of the stage after one of our many productions. There were only three African American students, but as I look at the smiles including mine, culture and race was not an issue. Attached to the Photograph is a note that I have saved and savored for the last twenty years. *Dear Mrs. McDonald, Next year I will miss you a whole bunch, but I'm very happy for the second graders that get the privilege of being in your class. I just loved, third grade with you being my teacher. Maybe we can write to each other. But thanks again for all you have done for me, your former student, Kate Nelson.*

I'm definitely going on a quest to find Kate, who should now be twenty seven or twenty eight years old. I would like for her to know how much I treasured our relationship and how much I would love to see her again. I wonder if she's married and has a little girl that looks just like her. With the internet, I'm certain that one day I will be able to hit her up on face book or even press the green button on my cell phone and hear her sweet voice on the other end.

I must include the picture of the first *Relay for Life Event:* that happened while teaching at Snow Hill Elementary School. Since that weekend in May, 1995, every year for at least fifteen years, my family has participated in these exciting activities. From the beginning, I encouraged schools (parents and staffs) to raise thousands of dollars for cancer research. Little did I know that just a few years later, I would have Breast Cancer: By God's Grace and Mercy I have been a survivor for twelve years.

A recent production on the Public Broadcasting Station (PBS), featured the life of William Lloyd Garrison who was an abolitionist during the 1880's. He gave most of his adult life to the fight against slavery in the south. How ironic it is as I reflect upon my relocation to Georgia, that my first school was named Garrison Mill Elementary School. A large painting hung on the wall in the front hall displaying proudly a hero of the south. The irony of this situation is that again, I was the only African American teacher, and although this was 1995, I was chosen to be a freedom fighter.

Just as I experienced on *The Hill Top,* years ago, parents and other teachers who were critical of my ability to teach Caucasian students. In this circumstance, however; I was older, more mature, and I had recently earned my Masters Degree in Education. I had also joined *The Beulah Baptist Church* in *Decatur* where the *Rev. Jerry D. Black* is the dynamic pastor and had several prayer partners. As my mother always told us, *you have to stay prayed up:*

Delta's of Beulah Baptist Church (1995)

Before finally retiring after ten years in the **Cobb County School System,** I had the opportunity to teach in another unique location. Big Shanty Elementary School was named after the **Battle of Big Shanty,** which was a famous Civil War Battle. Again, I was the only African American classroom teacher, however; Carolyn Hall was given the opportunity to become the first African American Principal at this school.

Technology was just being introduced into the classrooms as an excellent supplemental strategy to reinforce skills. Of course, you guessed it, I applied for an **A T & T Grant** and received one for a *$1,500.00.* My proposal paired senior high students with my kindergarten students and was a great success. (We even made the **Cobb County Education News**). The *Key Pals* as they were known became friends through this process and actually published an Anthology of Poetry. (I still pull out my copy and reminisce about those happy days).

I was extremely blessed to have as my paraprofessional at Big Shanty a beautiful spirit named Christie. I saved this note that she wrote to me when I transferred to Addison to become the first African American in Gifted Collaboration. Here is an excerpt from it: *Dearest Jewel, I want to thank you from all the corners of my heart, for being my friend, my mother, my sister and my guardian angel. I once thanked Carolyn for bringing Jewel to me . . . . a gem on the face of the earth!. I meant every word of it. I am sorry that I will not be your RIGHT HAND MAN this year. If I can be half the teacher you have been in your life, I will soon be Teacher of the Year! I have loved your gentle ways with the children—love shone through their eyes and yours. God blessed my life with you and your friendship! Much love, Christie.*

The last time that we saw each other, she had become a second grade teacher. I pray that our paths will cross again soon.

My last six years of teaching were as a *Student Support Specialist at Birney Elementary School.* It was my first experience in Georgia where the school and staff was completely integrated. While there, I was chosen to become a part of the first Diversity Council for the school district. I was blessed to be on the ground floor of diversity training in the Cobb County School District. I am proud to say along with LaVerne Suggs, Marquita Gilmer and others on the council, we were successful in promoting multicultural education. It was exciting to participate in events all over the county

We were living in Kennesaw at this time and decided to *join Kennesaw Avenue Missionary Baptist Church.(KAMBC).* **Rev. Richard E. Spann** is not only an excellent preacher of the word, but also prolific teacher of the Bible. For almost twenty years, Bobby and I never missed Tuesday Night Bible Study. Under Pastor Spann's leadership, I became a member of the Media Committee which produced a quarterly Newsletter, (*The KAMBC Press).* As the Health Editor, I researched several articles to enlighten the congregation concerning issues such as diabetes and lupus.

I miss being a part of such a vibrant, alive and spiritual environment. Now that we've moved to Riverdale, I'm over an hour away, however; Pastor Spann explained to me that no matter how far away I move, he **will always be my pastor. I've visited several churches in this area, but none are like KAMBC!**

September (2005) Parenting and Education is the headline on the article written a few months after the exciting retirement reception attended by hundreds. Under the headline was the title of the article

written by Laura Agadoni. LOCAL TEACAHER RETIRES AFTER 47 YEARS TEACHING:

It was an honor to have a reporter come to my home to interview me about what I had loved doing all my life. An except reads: *a fellow educator Iris said, Jewel is truly an inspiration to any aspiring or veteran educator. Her dedication emits from her perpetual commitment to children and colleagues.*

My best friends from Cleveland, Ohio came for my retirement after 47 years as an educator: (Yvonne and Ruth Ann, sitting in kitchen with me, 320 Ethridge Drive, Kennesaw, Georgia (2005).

Bobby and Elton are relaxing at the house on Edgewood Avenue in Cleveland, Ohio after an afternoon service. I know they are singing together in that heavenly choir..

(2010) THE REHAB: EXPERIENCE: AFTER BACK SURGERY:

You leave the hospital, wondering what the next three weeks will bring. Arriving at the Rehab Center at eleven o'clock P.M. in an ambulance, still in major pain and having all kinds of thoughts. The words of the doctor and therapist were so encouraging and optimistic. Being wheeled into my home for the next three weeks and hugging Bobby Good Bye, I settled in and tried to get a good nights rest.

The Rehab Experience was more than the intense physical therapy as you learned how to move through the pain and endure *Rehab Food,* you thank God for a wonderful roommate, nurses and therapists who are really angels. One of the special angels name was Esther and as God ordained it, we ended up having a Bible Study several nights at eleven when she came on duty.

I was told that I would be in rehab for six weeks, but I made it out in three. *What does that tell you?*

The most special part of the Rehab Experience was meeting someone who has become a wonderful friend and sister. It has been over a year since we met, and we have been together constantly. Her name is Patricia, but she's known to everyone as Pal. This is the perfect name for her as we have had exciting adventure after adventure.

Visiting her home was one of our first adventures. She had explained her family's love of animals, but I was not really prepared as we were greeted at the door by an enormous friendly dog, who almost knocked me over. He was only one of the four dogs, a cat, a bearded dragon, a lizard and a Boa Constrictor. Rasheed, Nasir and Malaan watched in awe at each animal in their own glass enclosed cages. During our many visits, Rasheed and Nasir finally held the lizard. Malaan and I have never been so brave.

One of the highlights of my stay in rehab was a visit from one of my special friends. Tomi Johnson and I taught together at Garrison Mill Elementary School when I first came to Georgia and remain close even though we don't get to see each other very often. She gave me **"Jocelyn**

Elders, M.D.'s book, *From Sharecropper's Daughter to Surgeon General of the United States of America.* As I read her life story, I realized how much it was like my own story. I read it early in the morning and late at night when I could not sleep.

Reading her story reminded me of when we traveled to Marianna, Arkansas to attend the Home Going Service of Mom's oldest brother Uncle James. On our way back to the hotel, on this very cold winter evening, we passed cotton field after cotton field, finally; we couldn't resist. We parked the car on the side of the road, climbed over the small fence and Delbert, Irene and I actually picked some cotton to take back home to show everyone I (I even put some in the Science Center in my Second/Third Grade Classroom), Of course this was the first time they had seen genuine cotton. *WHAT A TEACHABLE MOMENT!*

As I finished reading and comparing my life with "The Sharecroppers Daughter", I discovered that another strong bond connects us together. Not only are we a part of the great sisterhood of Delta Sigma Theta Sorority, but when she was walking around the campus *of Philander Smith College*, she was treading the hallowed ground of my sweet *Daddy Payne.* I found out later that he and his sister were the first in our family to graduate from a Historical Black College.

Later we also learned from our family historian, that Daddy Payne was also the first African American to enter *Julliard School of Music.*

During our first Family Reunion in Little, Rock, our cousin Lynette, took us to visit the campus. There are no words to describe the mixed feelings. There were feelings of joy and sadness, wishing that somehow we could have been there with our dear ones as they made their *footprints in the sands of time.*

Speaking of making footprints in the sands of time, I must mention my great-nephew Jamari Paramore Morgan. He's the son of my niece Jessica.

Jessica has always been extra special. She has a beautiful voice that she has shared in many venues. Not only did she graduate from Wilberforce University, a (HBC) fulfilling one of her dreams, she now is making us proud of her accomplishments as an union negotiator in corporate America.

Above the photograph in the sports section of **The Columbus Ohio Dispatch Newspaper,** the caption reads: *A Matter of huge proportions: 300 pounders a rare find, and for a good reason:* This was the scene as he completed his high school education. (2010), he has now completed two years in college football. To say that we are proud of Jamari's success on the field is nothing compared with our pride in his commitment as a Christian role model for his younger cousins and friends.

FROM KENNEDY TO OBAMA: 1960-2008

The lines were long, and excitement was in the air on a cold, rainy Tuesday afternoon in November, for the girl child from Marianna, Arkansas. Finally old enough to vote-this was a great time in my history and the history of our country. He was tall, handsome and would be the youngest president of the United States. As I listened to the results and realized that I had helped elect John F. Kennedy, I could only wonder would I live to help elect a black president.

In 2008, it's a different November afternoon. The sun is shining brightly— long lines are down the street, wrapped around buildings, and around corners. The city is now Marietta, Georgia not far from the **Macafee House** which years ago was a safe haven for the confederate army. This is also a special time because Malaan, my one year old granddaughter is sitting on my lap and I am now voting for the first African American President.

(She is holding a children's book. The title is *Yes We Can!* and every time she sees President Obama's picture, she raises her little fist and shouts, *Yes We Can!* We wonder what greatness is in her future.

January, 2013, President Obama is inaugurated again. It is an unusual experience as I watched the replaying of *Roots,* by **Alex Haley** the night before and realizing how far we as **African Americans** have come in the *United States of America.* I also look at my own history from (1936 to 2013) I would not be sitting in my study, safely, writing my autobiography had it not been for God's grace and merc

As I look out my window in Riverdale, Georgia, I also know that in the 1880's, this was the spot of a plantation and several slave cabins. I remember these words of a gospel hymn that we sang as a child. *We've come this far, by faith, leaning on the Lord. Trusting in His Holy name, He's never failed us yet.*

Argosy University—Atlanta Campus
College of Psychology and Behavioral Sciences
Doctor of Education, Pastoral Community Counseling
(EdD)

In May, 2012, I began the journey to acquire my Doctoral Degree in Pastoral Community Counseling. It has been almost a year, and the road has not always been easy, but as God promised, He has been with me every step of the way.

> *"Jewel, warm like wool—nature to*
> *nurture, "Water Dem Flowers-*
> *Maintain and empower. Devour a position: love conquers: any*
> *Blessings linked to you are plenty:"*
> *"Five cents for every life touched—means*
> *more than every life that*
> *Fuss." Sunshine describes your aura, like tulips describe beauty."*
> *Children pure as drivin snow, unconditionally—*
> *so the truth you must be as:*
> *Martin and Malcolm "ya see." Please be "The Solid Rock" you are*

And shift your weight to the one that
you're connected to by a star—
Near or far:
Presented to me by the author: (Rainbow
Sister) Geneva, Gaskins.

I still have fond memories of a special Saturday morning in August, 1989. The screams of pride and joy are still just as fresh, as my many friends and family members applaud as my name is called. Jewel Marie Williams McDonald is now receiving her Masters Degree in Education. Twenty four years later my plans are to participate in an all class reunion. In October, I will join other alumni from near and far and from many professions to help students recognize the opportunities that are available.

Founded in 2001, The *African American Alumni Society,* was originally formed to commemorate the 30th anniversary of the Bolinga Black Cultural Resources Center. While a student at Wright State University, I would have welcomed an organization such as this. At this time, there were very few people of color on campus. In all of my classes, I was always the only African American student, until my last few classes. I'm excited about attending this great event and in the words of Pat Jones, president of the alumni society, *It's important for us to reach out to our young people and help them achieve the goals that we have achieved and to even go further than that.*

The last week of July, 2013, will also be a week of celebration. Thousands of members of Delta Sigma Theta Sorority will gather in Washington D.C. to commemorate one hundred years. News Reporters from all over the world will excitedly show the beauty of a sea of red and white.

Homage will be paid to the twenty two founders who with courage and faith in God, marched for the right to vote. They also joined in other struggles faced by African American women in 1913. They were joined by such brave women as Mary McLeod Bethune who later founded Bethune Cookman College in Daytona Beach, Florida.

In October, 1957, on Ohio State University's campus, I became a member of this great sisterhood. Fifty five years later, I still actively participate and as a Delta Dear, I continually remind our young Sorors, *Only what you do for Christ will last.*

As a child growing up in the 1940's, The *Johnson Publishing Company was* an important part of our lives. As written in the *Special Issue: November 1992: 50 Years of JPC,* I felt that I was an integral part of this celebration. I was nine eight years old when on November 1, 1945 *Founding of Ebony Magazine marked the beginning of a new era in Black oriented Journalism.*

This statement is made in the article: *50 Events*

That Changed Black America.

I feel so blessed to live during all fifty events. As an educator one of the events that is mentioned and that I vividly remember: number 21: 9/22/57: *Nine Little Rock, Ark. schoolchildren are escorted to Central High School by federal troops, ending efforts to thwart court-ordered integration.*

Little did I know that next year and foe many years, I would be required to help integrate several schools. (*I had mixed emotions when during the 2005 Family Reunion, I was able to sit on the steps of the school which at that time had begun predominately African American*).

Another significant event that was listed as number 37, happened on November 7, 1967. *Carl Stokes of Cleveland, Ohio and Richard Hatcher of Gary Indiana become the first blacks elected mayors of major U.S. cities.* Not only was I thrilled about voting for Cleveland's first Black mayor, but just a month early my beautiful daughter Caryn was born. Then a few weeks later, I had the privilege of shaking his hand when he visited Captain Arthur Roth Elementary School where I was teaching kindergarten. I do still have the picture of him attending Greater Abyssinia Baptist Church one Sunday morning. He, Mayor Carl Stokes, is pictured with Pastor, Rev. E. T. Caviness. This picture can be seen on Page 54.

Although I retired as a *Public School Educator* nine years ago, I truly believe that when God called me to at age nine it was a calling that would last my entire life. When someone gave me a copy of <u>One World, One Heart,</u> written by, Susan Polis Schutz, I found the following message. I thought, WOW, she must have written this just for me.

When you interact with children, you must always keep in mind that everything you do and say has an enormous impact on their lives. If you treat children with love and respect, it will be easier for them to love and respect others. If you treat children with freedom and honesty, it will be easier for them to develop confidence in their abilities to make decisions. If you treat children with intelligence and sensitivity, it will easier for them to understand the world. If you treat children with happiness, kindness, and gentleness, it will be easier for them to develop into adults capable of enjoying all the beautiful things in life:

To all those women who have been blessed to have a <u>Sister/Friend,</u> you will understand what I'm writing about below. I had just retired from forty seven years in education, but was not ready to retire from teaching.

The following note that was sent to me was written when I opened the C.R.P. Center for Language Arts in 2006. I have read it over so many times. Times when I needed comfort, times when I needed comfort, times when I was sad and times when I just wanted to remember these words from my sister /friend.

God placed us in each other's lives at a Monday Night choir rehearsal. How ironic that a few years later, the most special love of my life entered my life at a Monday night rehearsal and stayed there until his dedeath forty years later.

To my sister/friend;

I am so excited for you! Congratulations! On the rest-and best-of your career life. It is only fitting that your retirement "profession" mirrors your life-long profession. I believe you to be the epitome of an educator . . . from an era when being a teacher was a profession of honor, dignity, respect and prestige. thank you, Sister for keeping that precious image alive. Though I've never had the good fortune to sit under your tutelage in a classroom, you have been my "spiritual" mentor from the first day we met. Be encouraged . . . and continue to encourage others with your love and guidance. Keep that spirit of "nevertheless" (Num.13:26-33). (28b) Nevertheless, the people be strong that dwell in the land: The best is yet to come-and remember that all things are possible with God:

Von:

Dear Von,
From your Sister/Friend,
Love Always,
Jewel

*A boy child (Bobby Jr.) entered our lives. The square is
filled with excitement and adventure. Every summer an
arm or a leg in a caste as the boy-child is never still:*

Season's Greetings

The Abraham's
Harland, Lisa,
Brandon & Jordan

Carrie R. Payne after retirement from the Bureau of Unemployment Compensation.

Caryn with her "Spec" as she becomes a Delta. (Howard University, Spring-1987

Columbus Public Schools

Columbus  Ohio

East High School
This Certifies That
Jewel Marie Williams

having satisfactorily completed a course of study prescribed for this High School, is awarded this

Diploma

Given this eleventh day of June, nineteen hundred fifty-four.

Austin Berensou
Principal

Homer Trantham
President of Board

N. H. Fawcett
Superintendent

Drake
Clerk of Board

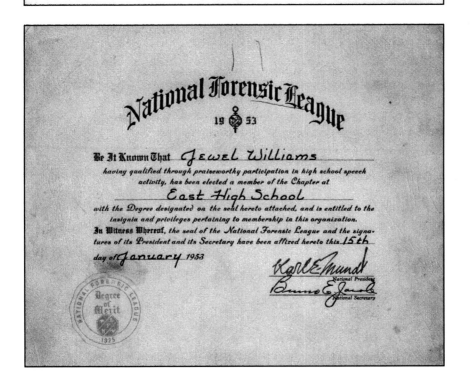

National Forensic League
19 · 53

Be It Known That *Jewel Williams*

having qualified through praiseworthy participation in high school speech activity, has been elected a member of the Chapter at

East High School

with the Degree designated on the seal hereto attached, and is entitled to the insignia and privileges pertaining to membership in this organization.

In Witness Whereof, the seal of the National Forensic League and the signatures of its President and its Secretary have been affixed hereto this *15th* day of *January* 1953

Karl E. Mundt
National President

Bruno E. Jacob
National Secretary

Degree of Merit

STOP, LOOK, AND LISTEN!

 The Carrie R. Payne Center For Language Arts!
Jewel M. McDonald CEO and OWNER:

WHO? *Boys and Girls (ages 4-7) Grades Pre-K – Second*

WHAT? *Reinforcement and Enrichment in Language Arts:*

   (Reading, Writing, Spelling)

WHEN? *Tuesday – Thursday*

TIMES? *Morning hours: 9:00 –1:00 A.M. Afternoon hours: 3:00 – 6:00 P.M.*

HOW? *Individualized, direct instruction using a variety of strategies; on going assessment and evaluation will guide appropriate instruction: Parents will be made aware their child's progress on a regular basis.*

WHERE: *We will be open to serve children in the cities of Acworth, Cherokee, Kennesaw, Marietta and other surrounding areas in Cobb County.*

If you would like to know more about the C. R. P. Center For Language Arts, call me at 404-723-0211 or e-mail me at jewelmcdonald@bellsouth.net. I'm looking forward to speaking with you soon.

HOW MUCH? To receive services will cost students $30.00 an hour. 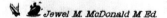 Come by land, sea or sky! We'll have a great time.

Jewel M. McDonald M Ed.

Grand Opening of Carrie R. Payne Center for Language Arts.

"Morsey" standing in front of 374 Kendall Place in the seventies.

Jewel's 50th birthday celebration in Columbus, Ohio: seated,
Jewel, Mom and Blonzetta, standing, Evelyn and Irene

*At the Governor's Mansion, 4th of July Celebration, Mom sang in
the choir. (Jewel,Governor Gilligan and Mom Carrie).*

*(Left to right, younger sister, Evelyn, twelve, older sister Jewel
age Twenty/living room , McCoySt. After church*

Two more events were especially significant, for different reasons but had a great impact on my life.

Number 36: October 2, 1967, Thurgood Marshall becomes the first black member of the U. S, Supreme Court, and through the power of television.

Number 44, September 20, 1984—The Cosby Show premiered on NBC-TV And changed the image of African Americans and the viewing habits of White Americans

Thanks to my brother and friend Imhotep Kuumba for allowing me to conclude with an excerpt from his poem.

Title of book: Slave Name
Name of poem: Like Memories of You
Author: Imhotep Kuumba
Excerpt from poem:
Somethings are forever like time and the change of weather and memories sure last a long time.
No guarantee on tomorrow, good times, happiness, pain and sorrow are all a part of life.

CPSIA information can be obtained at www.ICGtesting.com
Printed in the USA
LVOW06*0748140415

434460LV00003B/23/P

9 781466 976511